Aoife Mannix

ALICE UNDER THE KNIFE

SurVision Books

First published in 2021 by
SurVision Books
Dublin, Ireland
Reggio di Calabria, Italy
www.survisionmagazine.com

Copyright © Aoife Mannix, 2021

ISBN: 978-1-912963-26-3

This book is in copyright. No part of this publication may be reproduced, stored in a retrieval system, or transmitted in any form or by any means without the prior permission in writing from the publisher.

Acknowledgements

Grateful acknowledgement is made to the editors of the following, in which some of these poems, or versions of them, originally appeared:

Abridged: "What You Didn't Say," "Come Home," and "Still Life"

Bang! poetry: "Nearly-Nine Minutes"

Fortune Telling anthology: "Survivor"

Gargoyle: "Simple Directions"

The Honest Ulsterman: "Alice under the Knife"

Too Young, Too Loud, Too Different (Poems from Malika's Poetry Kitchen) anthology: "Fire"

"Not Letting Go" was part of One Stage at a Time digital/live performance, Arts Council of England

"Bifrost" appeared in Mary Evans Picture Library

"After Easter" was runner-up in the Welsh Poetry Competition 2018

For Dylan

Contents

Alice under the Knife	5
What You Didn't Say	6
Come Home	7
Fire	8
After Easter	10
Still Life	12
Simple Directions	13
Not an Invitation	14
Scarecrow Running	16
Thursday Evening	17
What Will Remain	22
Portrait	24
Survivor	26
After Square One	27
Premonition	28
Stung	29
Five Years	30
Not Letting Go	31
Pandemic	32
Ninety-Nine Minutes	33
Foreign	34
Bifrost	35
Cleopatra in Wuhan	36
Reflection	37

Alice under the Knife

I run into the blue. The woods are empty now of bird song
and the roses under the window back when kisses came in a box,
soft centred, deep. My footprints in the dust, scarlet blossom
whirling in water, a small animal slipping into an ice queen spring.
The Mad Hatter counts the seconds till it becomes too much.
I hide deep inside your teacup. Starvation my invisibility cloak.

When they cut out my womb, the hole in the lake creaked
with laughter. They removed my mother's cancer
along with my breasts. Futterwack dancer,
the Jack of Hearts, that knave, that stealer of summers,
swirled in a poker blizzard. They say I don't remember
but a coma is a different country. Full of falling pianos,
caterpillar smoke. Scars in the snow, my body
lost in calligraphy, haunted by Yetis with eyes of stone.

Too big, too small, they hand out their *eat me drink me* pills
flushed violet with panic, night sweats. Side effects of vanity.
Too late whispers the white rabbit, far too late.
His gold watch accusing as I struggle to sit up in the bed.
Hospital mirrors. Off with her head.

The forget me not blue winks between broken fingers
as I disappear down the hole in my shoe. Nobody escapes
the sudden chill of a lead morning when the words
break their wings against a cruel sky, the murder of crows.
Yet the jabberwocky wind in my mouth speaks of a shared grief,
a wonderland. The heels of a fox vanishing into tall grass.

What You Didn't Say

The road is silent, white ice
creaks beneath our boots.
Unsafe secrets. The violence
you can't articulate. Putting the latch
on the front door. The moaning of pipes.
Twenty years since I realised I'd never have
your courage. This birthday when you knew
you were dying. I eat my frozen pills,
agree to be anaesthetised. My whole body
threatens snow. Knives sharpen.

You said I'd get over it but maybe,
after all this time, it's not so much fear,
as the millennia of missing you.
If there were words for your gunshots to the head,
I haven't got the right questions. Just holding
your hand as you step out on to the ice.
The empty rooms echo with the deja vu
of drowning. We have been here before.

Come Home

You do not have to wear
these different voices,
the stranger on the telephone,
the shout over the wall.
Our house is fragments of rooms,
shattered glass from a falling lamp.
The light left on overnight.

Outside has become a different country.
Frosted wonder painted thickly
across the hill as the early morning sun
signs its name along my tongue.
There will be no more tattoos.
The challenge of being broken
into pieces, learning this new language
of isolation, how to navigate distance.

I set sail across the kitchen floor,
fearing the edge of translation.
There are such silences between us.
I want to write welcome in the window
even if the door is stripped naked,
closed until further notice.

Fire

I break into my neighbour's house.
It is derelict since she burnt it down last summer
in a fit of fire engines and exploding windows.

There are letters piled in large stacks.
My son stands behind me. We both know
this place is haunted. I examine the pipes,
the whistle of their reflected sorrow.

I'm sorry I stopped writing to you.
I know you dreaded a telephone call
but somehow your theories on how to avoid
other people's dreams became personal.

I wanted you to listen to white rooms
waiting for knives. You locked yourself up
in a French house on a cliff
claiming you were rehearsing.
I clung on by my fingernails.
Days of tedious pain.

My son wants to hang his dream catcher
in the window so he can hold on to the dark
that slips through his fingers.

We are burglars playing at arson.
My neighbour has disappeared.
My skin is scabbed with ghosts.

I wake to watch my son sleeping.

The perfect bow of his lips.
He is yawning in the language of those
who don't yet realise where this real life begins.

You never did know how to deal with insomnia,
death, the suffering of strangers you once loved.

After Easter

The sun returns.
Shy but confident
in the crown of a daffodil
dressed up as a king,
going to a party with pirates
and superheroes swinging
in a tree house by the owl's island.
Far from the icy rain
of relentless missiles falling
on foaming children
who have no answers to questions
they should never have to ask.

Ariel burns inside her tree.
Her branches not touching
but touched by yellow leaves
too old to know better,
as the birds rebel in their innocence.
Their songs humming in the wind
as if this April were the first resurrection.
These green shoots unsullied,
not twisted in the damp roots
of a hunger so deep
it swallows half the world.

The white blossom in a halo
of green rises up
over the edge of the hill.
Blackbirds celebrate
a morning freshly pressed

as clean sheets on a bed
where you are sleeping,
curled up like a small bear.
Nothing prepared me for
the length of your eyelashes.

Nothing prepared me for
the drone of an aeroplane
skimming the roof tops.
The bombs whisper down
on other people's children.
You say you want to live forever,
like a Time Lord or Jesus.
Your face is the last chocolate egg
hidden in my jewellery box.
I want to promise you
I will always come back,
but I am afraid
of the holes in my hands.

Still Life

My body has no tattoos,
just bumpy tracks branded into skin
that follow their own snakes through
shaded forests where the light
is sewn with the taste of iron.

It creaks in the mornings,
a door on rusty hinges
opening so slowly
to forgotten birdsong laced
with the poison of brittle bones.

But by mid afternoon
that back to front tightness
is smoothed by blood burbling
through a stream where a young girl
does not care she is drowning.
Wasted mirrors, the gift
of muscle and milk.

In the evenings I trace my scars,
draw maps of my missing breasts,
wonder if God still drinks wine,
or has left to travel the world
as a photographer of corpses.
I try to remember I am not
afraid of needles, invisible ink
writing your name upside down.

Simple Directions

Take your purple ukulele and tune in
to letting it go as you check the timetable
once more, not forgetting that the schedule
changes with the coming and going of children,
the chasing of foals across a field.
One of them rolling on his back, feet kicking the air
as you spot the single decker weaving round the bend.
Remember how you worried how long it would be
till you'd be well enough to make this journey again.
Pay your money and listen to the weather songs of old women
as a strange man offers you sweets. Settle into glimpses of sheep,
the castle with its music room, until you reach the cross
from the nursery rhyme. The lady on her fine horse
cast in bronze and clicking her heels. Ding the bell
and alight with thank yous before turning back
the way you've come past the pub of broken dreams
and the Polish surprise eggs till you reach the corner
with the money machine and the iconic public toilets.
Turn right into the howling glitter ball wind
and the endless scaffolding. Ring the lower door
and identify yourself as a collector, not a kidnapper.
Listen to a warm review of wolf dancing in French
before walking past jigsaw puzzles, toy cash registers,
racks of small shoes, and into the inner sanctum
of the nursery where a little boy is listening to a story.
His face bursting into song when he looks up
to see you are here to take him home.

Not an Invitation

I found the monster when I was crossing
the parking lot. His diesel claws clicking
on sulphur. You said you couldn't smell it.
The tiniest lump of lemon tickled
my throat. I was tempted to wipe the screen
sterile. I went back to nothing, almost,
absolutely, definitely nothing.
It was the auburn anniversary
of a death I wish I had never seen.
The hospital doors were sore and bloodshot.
Eerily familiar. The sky promised
a soft summer of lemonade sherbet
sipped slowly. She said I was lumpy.
She said she was sorry my mother died.

I knew then I was not imagining
the ghost of an x-ray. The creature aches.
Sometimes I think he's left but he's still there.
A fingerprint of an accusation.
Just scans. She said best let go of Vegas,
best not to sit alone, best not to wait.
As many biopsies as you can take.
There's a phrase I never wanted to hear.
The doctor smelt of peaches. He nearly
apologised. I swallowed
my bruises. I had drunk an iceberg.
We sat in the car and cried.
The beast ate the locks. I tried to explain
we would need all of his teeth removed.

Strange that it took such savage dentistry
to taste that you love me. That the jungle
was all in my head. Only the tiger
is real though he sounds like the memory
of somebody else's dream. His mouth wide.
He's out there now, prowling along the ledge.
I wouldn't say we were friends, I wouldn't
say I'd invite him to tea, but there is
a puzzle to his beauty all the same.
A wildness. He has stripped us right back.

Scarecrow Running

We sweep past the stream into
the eye of our resolutions.
October blue in sync with ruby dog walkers,
the fresh question of scars regenerating.
Electric shocks slice open
all that I have put behind me.
Through the eye of the ruin I ghost myself,
my hand no longer in yours. A white feather
wisps into wet grass. If I was not here
to see the marmalade cat aspire to catch
the flutter of squirrel, the last butterfly of the season,
you waving from the throne of the apple tree.

Magpie secrets melt as my spine stretches,
cathedral smoke raising the roof of grouse.
Lost seagulls steal seed from the brown earth.
Hospital birdhouses remind me of summer regret
but now that question of whether they will ever return
is muted by a soft day, the shock of white wings
rising up against a slate of sky. The Viking wind
slivers over the sea. A banshee caws the fragility of bone.
But the children are singing in the church
and we give such thanks for the halo harvest
humming in our ears. Arms outstretched
for the resurrection of crows, afraid but flying.

Thursday Evening

I

The stiff chairs in torturous rows, shuffling
handkerchiefs, polished black shoes creaking,
the velvet trap of an open coffin.
She does not sleep or resurrect the bright
relief of such frozen discovery,
as a candle burns hot in the window.
The sting of boot polish and a wax mask
are holes in this parade of the living,
trooping across thin carpet, with music.
The night is swirls of shadows, with music,
sung for the drowning of her crushed wings
in a cage, to rattle Jerusalem,
kingdom of wailing walls and ticking bombs.

II

Why should she close the cell door behind her?
What is purgatory if not this room
where the undertaker softly explains
the challenges of parking after mass?
When she asked for help, she felt there was
something there for her beyond surgery,
beyond the profanity of doctors
and the old lies of chemotherapy.
She said, "if only there was time I'd find
a new religion, not in the Latin
of paedophiles and gross hypocrisy,
but in the healing stones of famine roads

where ghosts cross without ever looking twice.
Their repossessions economic jokes
your man on the cross would appreciate."

III

That three in one trick she couldn't repeat
or how can a mother stay a virgin
when Gabrielle goes clubbing with any
old whore who falls for his feather mattress?
She would have put him up for adoption
but the Holy Spirit poured her a drink
saying, "I can see your own reflection."
Still all those babies later she wanted
to know what was wrong with contraception?
Steps of a stairs, Irish twins, the blood of
miscarriages and altar wine. God may
forgive her but she's not so sure she wants
to forgive Him; her father Hamlet's ghost.
Nothing became him like disappearing
to a land of incurable heathens.

IV

She says, "I am bitter with false witness,
the heaven I was promised if only
I followed all the rules and kept my legs
crossed to love; the thin protection of phone
books and the priest telling us girls not to
come over too intelligent or we would
never get a husband; definition
of hell or irredeemable failure."
Is Paradise a semi-detached house

in the suburbs where your sister insists
she is the saint you could never achieve?
Is there no jealousy in the garden
of the apocalypse or are the four
horsemen in a pointless race to finish?
Guilt is filthy water for bathing in.

V

She says, "Now I am thrown on the mercy
of my daughters, I regret my prophets
because is it right that my sons are not
nursemaids but will carry my oak coffin?"
She tried to bend her prayers but broke them
on the promises of words unspoken
and the sickness she was forced to share.
Her fear that on the other side she'll find
there's no one waiting and the loneliness
of the truth is more than any mother could bear.
Mysterious cruelty; God's punch line
or a confession of wanting this faith
in spite of walking on women, papal
infallibility, crackpot science,
the fairy stories she longs to be true.

VI

Why does she have to die when there are still
so many songs she never got to sing?
What comfort is a golden harp upon
a fluffy cloud when a man in a long
white beard was the start of all her trouble?
Neither the shrill pips of the Angelus

before the news nor the bell that struck down
the swans nor Mary losing her only
child explained the need for all this pain
and addiction to suffering, but once
she stood in a church on Christmas Eve when
the hallelujah sparkled in the glass
windows and the notes shattered her body,
the chorus carried her on angels' wings
as she flew much higher than God himself.

VII

Now she lies in her coffin, the question
of whether she ever really liked
lilies, their pale moon faces mocking us
with the fact of there being no answer.
Whether they donate these flowers today
to the dying or burn them with her corpse,
the ashes cannot hear violin strings
snapping, the murmuring of broken voices
promising she is in a better place
with the sad implication there's nowhere
that's worse than a hospital bed; hell is
other patients, the ghosts haunting her dreams
with what she wishes she had said before
the curtains closed on all the living
when she slid into the coldest of fires.

VIII

In Bethlehem the bread is the body.
The three wise men bring no gifts for Mary
as virgin whore refugee suicide

bomber nailed to the cross of martyrs.
Only men are resurrected, can afford
to be the nonbelievers, the sky rains
missiles and Kalashnikovs that destroy
all the years it took to raise her children.
Death is ugly and unkind, we still live
in the dark of our convictions; thank God
for doubt which makes us feel the mystery
of the thinness of our skin; perhaps there
is no reality, perhaps the time
has come to confess we walk as shadows
singing hymns on a cold night without stars.

What Will Remain

After the zombie apocalypse, they will find
the remains of bright red plastic blocks
and imagine that the great Lego pyramids
of ancient Toysrus were so immense and vast
you could see them from the moon,
which in the olden days was something
to be howled at, chipped into silver coins
that were used as identity cards
in burial sites containing hundreds
of tiny cups and saucers
as well as enormous flags
sewn from plastic bags emblazoned
with the names of famous warriors
like Tesco and Lidl.

They will tell stories of tombs
full of small black boxes,
shiny and with no apparent purpose
but to beam back your own reflection.
They will sing of the adventures of Google
who searched the jungles
for nine hundred years
until all of the trees had died.

They will not remember us
but they might one day
unearth a ship's drawer
buried under the apple tree
which contains only

your blue drawing of a superhero
saving the world from bad guys.

The dreams of children will survive.

Portrait

Paint me October yellow with its hush of leaves
clinging to branches, its startling reds
that burn with the promise of winter.
Those last days when the trees haunt
an Atlantic sky. Weary guests at
a fancy dress ball, swaying with the wine
and the lateness of the hour.

Let me wear glass slippers
and hide inside the pumpkin mask.
The three faces carved in the window
with their lurid grins and flickering candles.
Scoop out my insides. Make me hollow
as a skeleton. Draw my bones in chalk.
And if you must show my scars,
let them be written on water
as it flows under the weeping willow,
a ghost of a signature.

I am not fond of mirrors,
photographs, harsh reflections.
I'd rather be that trick of the light
in the far corner of a room
that was possibly an accident
or once painted white.
Show me not as a still life
but pouring seed through my fingers.

A scarecrow of a girl,
something of a vampire,
someone who has eaten fireworks,
perhaps the tiniest hint of a smile.

Survivor

You hide out in the attic, ignoring the dirty dishes
rioting below, the dust that scratches in the corners,
the piles of rubbish by the front door, the doorbells
that ring into silence. You keep your clothes
in a plastic bag. Your wardrobe is scattered in pieces
like a broken raft. You sink into tired, toxic
sheets. The windows whisper old newspaper
headlines, yesterday's tragedies. The whistle
of a car alarm in the distance, somebody else's crime.
You stand accused of losing your own address.

Taking a different way home to avoid the traffic,
you pass the name of a saint painted on a wall.
The familiarity bothers you till you finally remember,
ah yes, you used to live on this street, a long time ago,
before you tried paint stripper on the past.
Underneath there are rocking horses, someone's childhood
just after the war. You ride the night like a changeling.
The rats in the walls have forgotten your name.

After Square One

The babble of the birds as they bowl over
the rush of a burbling stream
bearing small sticks and buzzing
with the riot of bees who are busy
brandishing their pollen headlines
as they be-bop-a-lula
to the beat of a burnt-out sky
bearing down on brown branches
waltzing to the beautiful balaclava bunnies
who burrow through an explosion
of poppies and belly slapping dandelions,
brisk and giving birth to petal bicycles
flying over the brow of the hill
as we breathe in the miracle
of being reborn into a barren world,
which is not between catastrophes
or holding its badgers in silence,
when there are babies boiling over
into the arms of mothers,
and the bountiful earth is bedazzling
with its bluest of blue skies,
and we are brilliant with spring,
the miracle of Boudicca, Botticelli,
all those trail blazers.

Premonition

I was cycling as a child
when dread gripped my handlebars.
Though the traffic was ordinary
and slow, I had in my bones
the conviction something terrible
had happened. I raced home,
rushing in covered in sweat
and panic, to find you in the kitchen
stirring the gravy for dinner.
You paused at my wild eyes,
frozen stock still for a moment,
like a photograph, before I insisted
it was nothing, nothing at all.

You died young of a disease
that spread through the years
till I was surgically slipping
through ice. Scared and alone,
I suddenly remembered,
nearly three decades later,
that moment when I did not understand
what was wrong. The wheels
spinning through a crack in time.
All that we can never know.

Stung

We were playing tug-of-war
in the garden. Pretending to lose,
I stepped back on to a bee.
I was barefoot, he was wearing
his jacket. Flew off rather shakily
as the shock set in. Had I signed
his death warrant? Later that afternoon
in the hospital with acute people
dying, I buzzed beneath my mask.
Thought of climbing inside a fox glove
where all would be translucent purple
and strong nectar. I needed a drink.
My toes had swollen.
It was the least of my worries.

Five Years

The summer the burglars stole
all the silver, my mother laughed
because now we had the insurance
to line the house with central heating.
But I was shocked by the tarnished door,
how strangers could rip holes
in the pockets of our clouds.

On this anniversary of walking
out of the hospital, fresh minted
with the memory of metal
in my blood, how the sky
glinted with the rub and polish
of surgery, endless private
and confidential invasion,
the echo of cancer.
How my body, just like my mother's,
was to have the drawers thrown open,
spoons rattling to the floor,
I remember to be grateful for the warmth.

Not Letting Go

There's been a plane crash
and I am one of the survivors
who make camps on a sheet of ice,
Antarctica perhaps.

There is a perfect circle cut in the snow.
I fall in thinking this is cold but it's okay
but then suddenly I am being sucked
down and down at great speed
and it's freezing but I'm thinking
I'll just go with it when suddenly
it occurs to me but what about my little boy,
this is far too cold for him.

So I start desperately trying to swim back up,
it's the most enormous effort
and then I realise I'm under the ice
and I need to find the hole if I'm to get out.

I hear someone talking on the phone
and I'm filled with rage because why
are they talking about me as if I'm not there
when I'm right here only I can't open my eyes.

I wake with the most disturbing feeling
that this has not been a dream,
this actually happened to me
on an operating table in a hospital
where I came back from a place
that was colder than anywhere I've ever known.

Pandemic

I am back in that box marked phobia of hospitals.
My lungs stripped of tinned cans of milk.
There is a preacher with a gun in Florida
who refuses to stop praying with his followers
flocked together in some weird cultish suicide pact
with the devil of the detail as the cops wonder
whether shooting is contagious.

We are standing on the edge of our lives
and the distances are too great and yet
not far enough. I thought I had escaped
these scars but every night I dream
you are kissing me. The curtains have closed
and the show cannot go on. The pain sneaks
back stage and questions whether there will be
money in the bank, a world to return to.

My skin fragile as the shell of an egg.
The birds sing louder now we have
fallen silent. I am listening to the music
of apple blossom in a breeze sharper
than surgical knives. I am staying still,
camouflaged from oxygen, waiting
for the wolf to pass our door.

Nearly-Nine Minutes

The streets are on fire
with an anger that sits
in the throats of the silenced.
Shattered glass,
pepper spray tongues.
The words contagious
as they lick
along the skin.
A house so white
its fiddler has injected bleach
into the veins of a nation.
Poison behind the masks.
A police officer kneeling
on the neck of a black man.
How much murder can they
expect to get away with?

Foreign

The fox gloves stretch high as the shed window,
clapping their claws in a shock of purple velvet,
bumblebee teeth biting into the sky,
breaking the neck of the goose
for the sheer hell of it,
the perfect bell of their echo
in a secret language
I have never managed to learn.
If I had more names like snapdragons
I could breathe fire into a summer afternoon
but instead I am humming that tune
of a cold stream running deep under the bridge
into a country of speckled shadows.

Bifrost

The afterlife is not a place I've been,
even on those pillar of salt mornings
when the hush of Halloween mutes
the indigos and violets of our footsteps.
We trip trap across the bridge in its mist
of racing twigs. That blue-sky book
of Scandinavian demons, the ogre
on the roof, the trolls waiting for goats.
As a child, I curled in close to my mother
to breathe her fear of ice ghosts.

I wish I had a connection between this world
and the next but I dream in black and white.
There are no rainbows in my nightmares.
Only the cold and the fear of losing you
that whispers through the picture books.
You turned every page as if you knew
the inside of the lunatic asylum,
as if loneliness were a woman sat
in a chair by a window, staring out
at a fjord only she can see. The gods
hiding behind their mountains
and promising a very long way to fall.

Cleopatra in Wuhan

Snake streets in which love is stripped back
to a silent desert empty of soldiers.
You can have too much beauty.
I am queen of the deserted sky trains,
the roads that repeat their quarantine crossings.
Empires fall but this kiss of poison seeps back
across borders. When is it time to let go?
My skin slides free, curls into a question
of shoes, the cutting of hair. I wear my masks
in a city suspended, prisons in small boxes.

Reflection

Once more there are space rangers
in the sitting room, cardboard cities
carved by children. A glass raised
to the old haunted spaces.
You are all about the gift of haircuts
as you pack your goodbyes.
You don't hear the windows
in my fingerprints, how the horizon
has shattered. I hide in the shards
as I count five years of surviving
surgical exhaustion. It's all about
the knives, how much can be given,
how much can be taken away.

There are stones in my lungs.
Breathing is a conjuror's trick.
I am holding myself so still
inside this hall of mirrors.
Watch me walk out of the photograph.
How the light has lost my shadow.
A bubble rising up over the trees,
catching fire as the moon
shimmers in a blue sky.

Selected Poetry Titles Published by SurVision Books

Seeds of Gravity: An Anthology of Contemporary Surrealist Poetry from Ireland
Edited by Anatoly Kudryavitsky
ISBN 978-1-912963-18-8

Noelle Kocot. *Humanity*
(New Poetics: USA)
ISBN 978-1-9995903-0-7

Ciaran O'Driscoll. *The Speaking Trees*
(New Poetics: Ireland)
ISBN 978-1-9995903-1-4

Helen Ivory. *Maps of the Abandoned City*
(New Poetics: England)
ISBN 978-1-912963-04-1

John W. Sexton. *Inverted Night*
(New Poetics: Ireland)
ISBN 978-1-912963-05-8

Afric McGlinchey. *Invisible Insane*
(New Poetics: Ireland)
ISBN 978-1-9995903-3-8

Anatoly Kudryavitsky. *Stowaway*
(New Poetics: Ireland)
ISBN 978-1-9995903-2-1

Tim Murphy. *The Cacti Do Not Move*
(New Poetics: Ireland)
ISBN 978-1-912963-07-2

Clayre Benzadón. *Liminal Zenith*
(New Poetics: USA)
ISBN 978-1-912963-11-9

Thomas Townsley. *Tangent of Ardency*
(New Poetics: USA)
ISBN 978-1-912963-15-7

Matthew Geden. *Fruit*
(New Poetics: Ireland)
ISBN 978-1-912963-16-4

Marc Vincenz. *Einstein Fledermaus*
(New Poetics: USA)
ISBN 978-1-912963-20-1

Anton Yakovlev. *Chronos Dines Alone*
(Winner of James Tate Poetry Prize 2018)
ISBN 978-1-912963-01-0

Mikko Harvey & Jake Bauer. *Idaho Falls*
(Winner of James Tate Poetry Prize 2018)
ISBN 978-1-912963-02-7

Tony Bailie. *Mountain Under Heaven*
(Winner of James Tate Poetry Prize 2019)
ISBN 978-1-912963-09-6

Nicholas Alexander Hayes. *Amorphous Organics*
(Winner of James Tate Poetry Prize 2019)
ISBN 978-1-912963-10-2

John Bradley. *Spontaneous Mummification*
(Winner of James Tate Poetry Prize 2019)
ISBN 978-1-912963-13-3

John Thomas Allen. *Rolling in the Third Eye*
(Winner of James Tate Poetry Prize 2019)
ISBN 978-1-912963-15-7

Gary Glauber. *The Covalence of Equanimity*
(Winner of James Tate Poetry Prize 2019)
ISBN 978-1-912963-12-6

Charles Kell. *Pierre Mask*
(Winner of James Tate Poetry Prize 2019)
ISBN 978-1-912963-19-5

Alan Elyshevitz. *Mortal Hours*
(Winner of James Tate Poetry Prize 2020)
ISBN 978-1-912963-21-8

Henry Finch. *Reversing Falls*
(Winner of James Tate Poetry Prize 2020)
ISBN 978-1-912963-22-5

Jon Riccio. *Eye, Romanov*
(Winner of James Tate Poetry Prize 2020)
ISBN 978-1-912963-24-9

Alison Dunhill. *As Pure as Coal Dust*
(Winner of James Tate Poetry Prize 2020)
ISBN 978-1-912963-23-2

Anton G. Leitner. *Selected Poems 1981–2015*
Translated from German
ISBN 978-1-9995903-8-3

George Kalamaras. *That Moment of Wept*
ISBN 978-1-9995903-7-6

Order our books from https://survisionmagazine.com/books.htm